He was two and a half months old when he made them.

Tigers have large padded feet

that help them silently stalk their prey.

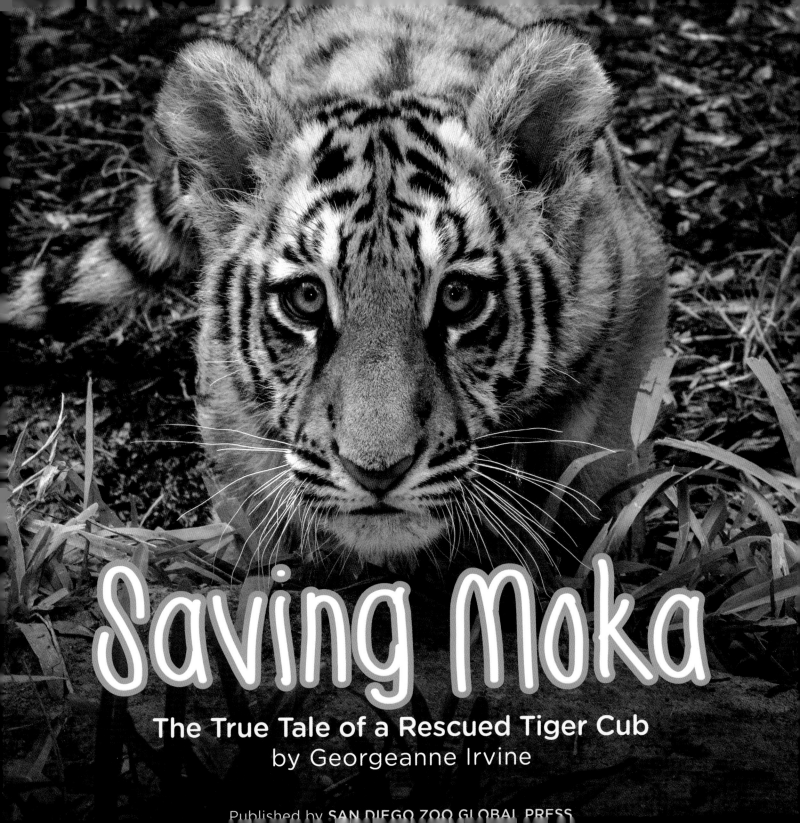

Saving Moka

The True Tale of a Rescued Tiger Cub
by Georgeanne Irvine

Published by SAN DIEGO ZOO GLOBAL PRESS

Saving Moka: The True Tale of a Rescued Tiger Cub was published by San Diego Zoo Global Press in association with Blue Sneaker Press. Through these publishing efforts, we seek to inspire multiple generations to care about wildlife, the natural world, and conservation.

San Diego Zoo Global is committed to leading the fight against extinction. It saves species worldwide by uniting its expertise in animal care and conservation science with its dedication to inspire a passion for nature.

Paul Baribault, President and Chief Executive Officer
Shawn Dixon, Chief Operating Officer
Yvonne Miles, Corporate Director of Retail
Georgeanne Irvine, Director of Corporate Publishing
San Diego Zoo Global
P.O. Box 120551
San Diego, CA 92112-0551
sandiegozoo.org | 619-231-1515

San Diego Zoo Global's publishing partner is Blue Sneaker Press, an imprint of Southwestern Publishing House, Inc., 2451 Atrium Way, Nashville, TN 37214. Southwestern Publishing House is a wholly owned subsidiary of Southwestern Family of Companies, Nashville, Tennessee.

Christopher G. Capen, President, Southwestern Publishing House
Carrie Hasler, Publisher, Blue Sneaker Press
Kristin Connelly, Managing Editor
Lori Sandstrom, Art Director/Graphic Designer
swpublishinghouse.com | 800-358-0560

ISBN: 978-1-943198-12-2
Library of Congress Control Number: 2020901884
Printed in Thailand
10 9 8 7 6 5 4 3 2 1

To Moka the tiger,
who survived in spite of a challenging beginning
to his life, and to all the women and men who
are fighting to stop wildlife trafficking.

Acknowledgments:

HEARTFELT THANKS TO ALL OF THE PEOPLE WHO HELPED BRING MOKA'S STORY TO LIFE AS WELL AS THOSE WHO HELPED SAVE HIS LIFE:

Ian Chatfield; Lissa McCaffree; Eileen Neff; Lori Hieber; Janet Lawhon; Katie Christofferson; Elise Montanino; Kimberly Millspaugh; Meredith Clancy, DVM; Lauren Howard, DVM; Jim Oosterhuis, DVM; Ryan Sadler, DVM; Randy Rieches; Autumn Nelson; Mike Mace; Mandi Makie; Jessica Flaherty; Lyndsey Nash; Peggy Sexton; Mary Thurber; Denise Carson; Anna Prigge; Steven Thurston; U.S. Customs and Border Protection: Angelica De Cima, Steven P. Bansbach, Jason T. Spencer, Shalene R. Thomas, Anne M. Sittmann, Brandon A. Montgomery, and Karina Leyva; U.S. Fish and Wildlife Service: Erin Dean and Christina Meister; Smithsonian's National Zoo and Conservation Biology Institute: Jennifer Zoon and Pamela Baker-Masson; Josh Jackson, DVM; Mary Sekulovich; Victoria Dunch; Victoria Garrison; Suzanne Hall; Ken Bohn; Tammy Spratt; Ryoko Chonan; Kim Turner; Lisa Bissi; Jen MacEwen; Angel Chambosse; and Yvonne Miles.

PHOTO CREDITS
Ken Bohn: 4 full page, 5, 9 upper, 10 lower, 11, 14 upper, 20, 22 lower, 29, 30, 31, 32 upper, 33, 34 lower right, back cover.
Ian Chatfield: title page, 7, 9 inset, 10 upper, 14 lower, 15, 16 left, 17, 18 right, 19, 21 lower, 22 upper, 23, 24, 25 upper, 26.
Tammy Spratt: front cover, front jacket flap, 3, 21 upper, 25 lower, 27. **U.S. Customs and Border Protection:** 4 inset, 6.
Smithsonian's National Zoo and Conservation Biology Institute: 12, 13. **Georgeanne Irvine:** 18 upper left. **Mary Thurber:** 28.
Ryoko Chonan: 32 lower. **Angel Chambosse:** back jacket flap. **Shutterstock:** 34 (except lower right), 35, 36.

Striped Surprise at the Border

A shiny silver sports car rolled to a stop at the U.S./Mexico border, just south of San Diego, California. The teenage driver and his friend were heading into the United States in the wee hours of a summer morning. The car's license plates looked suspicious to the U.S. Customs and Border Protection officer. So, he sent the vehicle to a second checkpoint where the driver could be questioned to make sure the car wasn't stolen.

Vehicle Inspection ↘

Inspeccion ↘ de autos

4

6

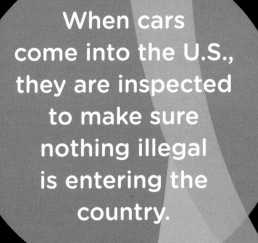

When cars come into the U.S., they are inspected to make sure nothing illegal is entering the country.

Using his flashlight, Officer Jason Spencer scanned the front and back seats looking for anything unusual. He was surprised to see a small cat lying on the floor between the passenger's feet. "It's just a special kind of house cat I bought for my girlfriend," said the man. Then the cat yawned and stretched as it looked up at Officer Spencer. That's when the officer knew it wasn't just a house cat—it was a baby tiger!

Officer Spencer realized the two men were trying to smuggle the tiger cub into the United States. Most likely, they planned to sell it illegally to someone who shouldn't have a tiger. While the men were being arrested, another officer took the cub out of the car and placed it in a big dog kennel where it would be safe. The tiny male tiger seemed friendly, as if he were used to being handled by people.

Officer Spencer

Later that morning, a U.S. Fish and Wildlife Service officer delivered the cub to the San Diego Zoo Safari Park hospital. It would live at the Safari Park until it was old enough to move to a permanent home at a wildlife sanctuary.

Smuggling wild animals into a country is called wildlife trafficking, and it is against the law.

Tiger Cub Checkup

Veterinarian Jim Oosterhuis examined the baby tiger. The cub chuffed at Dr. O as he listened to his heart, looked in his nose and ears, and drew blood. The tiger weighed a little more than six pounds, so Dr. O guessed he was between five and six weeks old. Dr. O was sad and concerned that the cub had been taken from his mother soon after he was born.

Chuffing is a friendly tiger greeting. It sounds like "fuff, fuff, fuff."

After the exam, keepers fed the hungry cub.
He quickly slurped down his milk formula and immediately fell sound
asleep. He was exhausted!

The tiger was moved to the Safari Park's Animal Care Center,
where he would be safe and have around-the-clock care. The keepers
quickly learned that the cub screamed when he was hungry or when
he wanted someone to play with him!

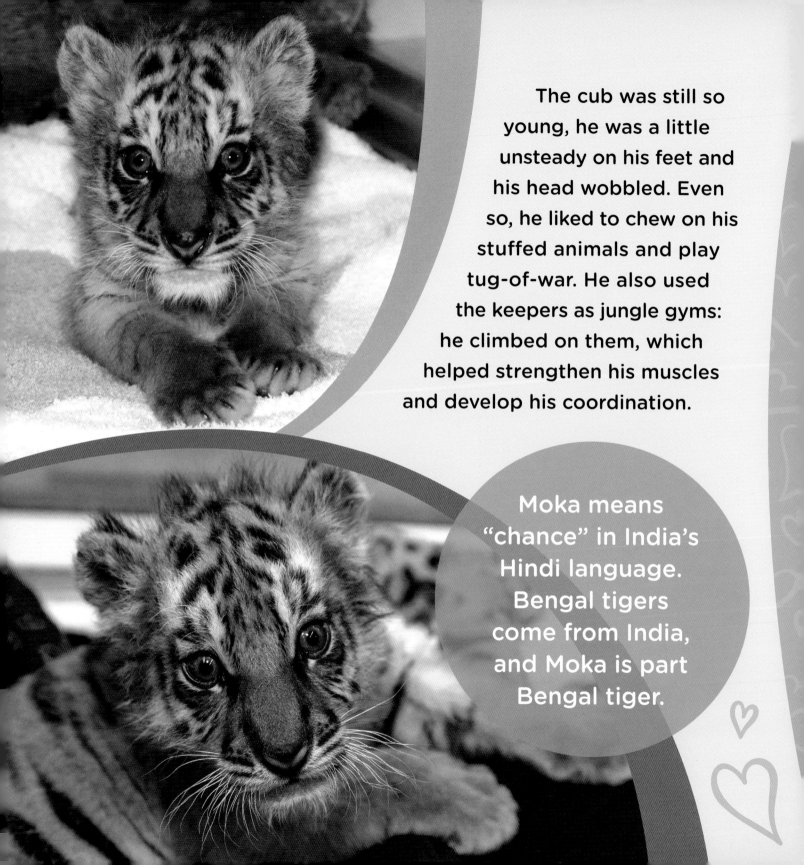

The cub was still so young, he was a little unsteady on his feet and his head wobbled. Even so, he liked to chew on his stuffed animals and play tug-of-war. He also used the keepers as jungle gyms: he climbed on them, which helped strengthen his muscles and develop his coordination.

Moka means "chance" in India's Hindi language. Bengal tigers come from India, and Moka is part Bengal tiger.

To calm Moka before nap time, his keepers played music. He liked rhythm and blues, nature sounds, and tunes from the Disney movie *Frozen*.

The keepers enjoyed playing with the cub, who was named Moka. They knew in their hearts, though, that the best thing for him would be to play with another tiger cub, especially because he wasn't with his tiger family.

Furry Friend for Moka

A few weeks after Moka arrived at the Safari Park, his keepers received surprising and exciting news. Moka was getting a playmate—another tiger cub close to his age.

An endangered Sumatran tiger cub was born at the Smithsonian's National Zoo in Washington, D.C. When he was six weeks old, his mother stopped caring for him. His keepers didn't know why his mother rejected her cub, but he would now need to be hand-raised by people. Staff at both zoos decided it would be best to raise the cubs together as brothers—at the Safari Park!

Within two days, keepers from the National Zoo fastened their seat belts on a Southwest Airlines jet bound for San Diego. The baby tiger rested comfortably in a small kennel that was strapped in a seat next to them.

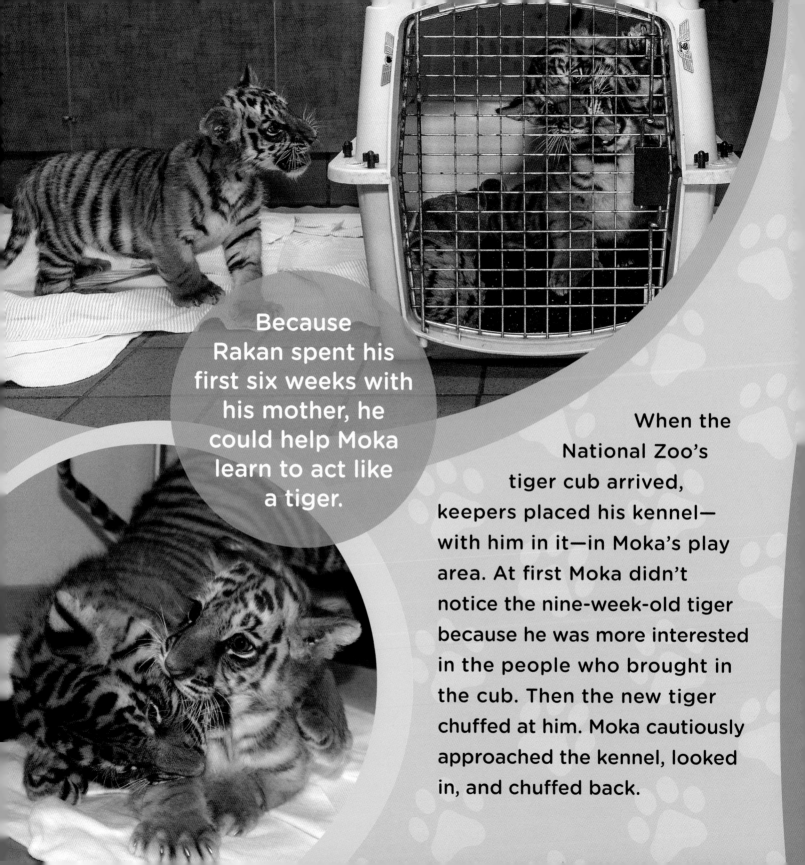

Because Rakan spent his first six weeks with his mother, he could help Moka learn to act like a tiger.

When the National Zoo's tiger cub arrived, keepers placed his kennel—with him in it—in Moka's play area. At first Moka didn't notice the nine-week-old tiger because he was more interested in the people who brought in the cub. Then the new tiger chuffed at him. Moka cautiously approached the kennel, looked in, and chuffed back.

When the kennel door was opened 30 minutes later, there was an instant tiger connection between the two cubs. They wrestled, batted at each other with their paws, growled, and then played chase around the room. The keepers were relieved that they got along so well.

Moka's new tiger friend received the perfect name: Rakan, which means "friend" in the Malay language.

Moka

You can tell the two tigers apart by their stripe pattern.

Rakan

Moka Might Be Sick

A week after the tiger cubs met, keeper Ian noticed mucus in Moka's pee. He took Moka to the Safari Park hospital, where a veterinarian examined him using an ultrasound machine. She saw that one kidney was bigger than the other. That meant Moka most likely had a kidney infection, so he was given medicine to make him well.

An ultrasound takes photos inside your body by using sound waves.

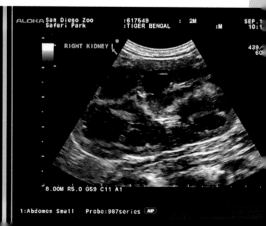

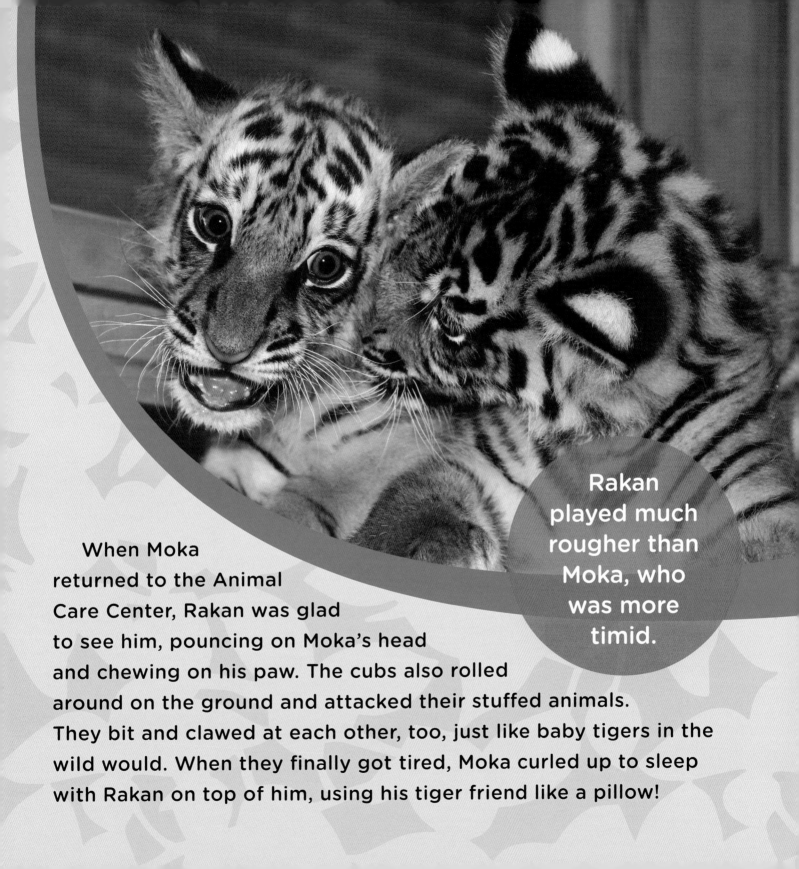

Rakan played much rougher than Moka, who was more timid.

When Moka returned to the Animal Care Center, Rakan was glad to see him, pouncing on Moka's head and chewing on his paw. The cubs also rolled around on the ground and attacked their stuffed animals. They bit and clawed at each other, too, just like baby tigers in the wild would. When they finally got tired, Moka curled up to sleep with Rakan on top of him, using his tiger friend like a pillow!

Moka and Rakan grew bigger and stronger. At 10 weeks old, Moka weighed 16 pounds and Rakan, who was two weeks older, weighed 19 pounds. The day the tigers jumped on the counter of their nursery room, the keepers knew it was time to move them to a larger living space at the Animal Care Center. They were also given access to an outdoor pen so they had more room to run and romp!

The cubs were wild about playing outdoors! They liked the new sights, sounds, smells, and toys. They roughhoused, tackled each other, and climbed on and in their drinkers. A favorite toy was a blue-and-white pool float, which they chewed on and carried around. They also dunked toys—and themselves— in a rubber tub filled with water.

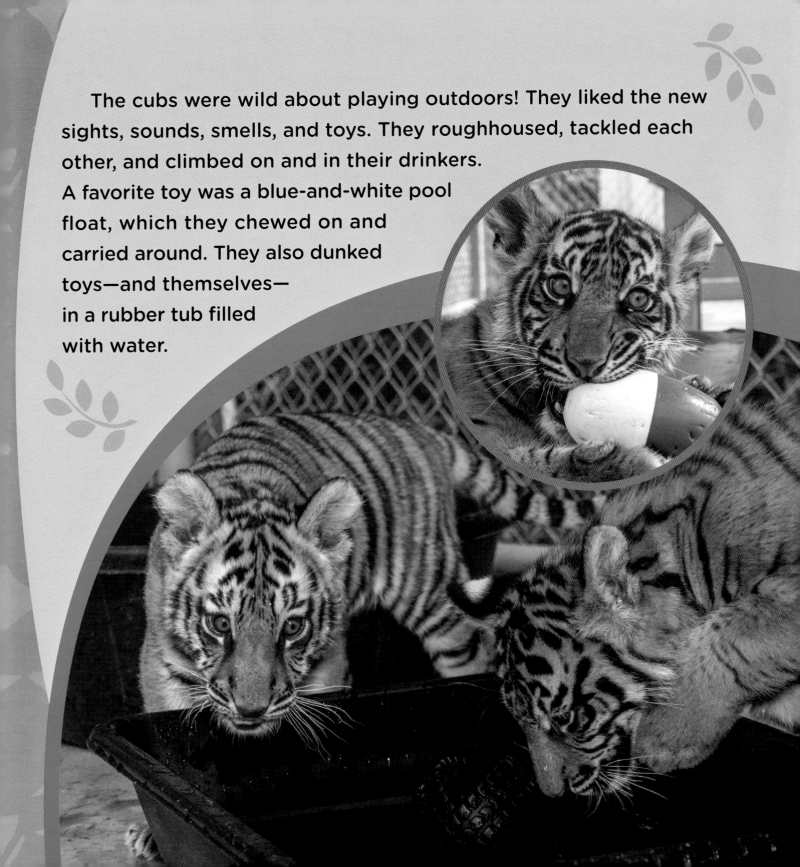

Playdates at Tiger Trail

After a few weeks of living in their larger space, Moka and Rakan would soon be leaving the Animal Care Center to live at the Tiger Trail habitat near the grown-up tigers. They wouldn't hang out in the same area as the adult tigers, but they would be able to see, smell, and hear them.

Before the move, Moka and Rakan went on playdates to Tiger Trail so they could slowly get used to it. For their first visit, keepers Ian and Jessica carried the cubs in a kennel into the lush green habitat. When they opened the kennel door, both cubs peered out, but brave Rakan took the first step into the unfamiliar area. He was uneasy and walked around slowly, looking at the logs, rocks, plants, and towering trees.

Keeper Ian talked softly to Moka, "Come on, big boy. Everything is all right." Then Ian chuffed at him. Within five minutes, Moka was exploring his new home, too.

After two weeks of daily visits to Tiger Trail, Moka and Rakan moved there to live full time. The cubs' new home was the perfect tiger playground.

Both cubs weighed 25 pounds and ate meat now. They were gaining about a pound per day!

A favorite game was stalking and ambushing each other. Rakan crouched behind a bush or log. When Moka walked by, Rakan leaped out and pounced on him, biting Moka on the scruff of the neck or leg. Moka screamed so Rakan would stop. Then Moka leaped onto Rakan and bit him! The tiger cubs weren't hurting each other—roughhousing is how all tigers play. It helps them build their muscles and strength.

Tiger School for Cubs

Targets, like the blue-and-white buoy, are used as training tools. The tigers will get a reward if they touch their nose or paw to the target when asked.

While Moka and Rakan were still small, they went to "tiger school." Their keepers spent a few minutes each day training them to do behaviors such as opening their mouth and coming when called. These behaviors would help the keepers and veterinarians take care of the tigers when they grow older and bigger. The cubs were good students—they were rewarded with meatballs and tiny pieces of beef heart.

As soon as the cubs were six months old, the keepers couldn't go inside the enclosure with them anymore because Moka and Rakan were too big and strong. However, they could work with them from behind a protective mesh wall. If a veterinarian needed to check the tigers' teeth or look at their paws, the keepers called Moka and Rakan to the wall. The cubs opened their mouth or lifted their paw when the keepers asked them to do so. Then the veterinarian could safely examine them.

Something Is Wrong with Moka

When Moka was seven months old, he started limping and holding up his left paw when he roughhoused with Rakan. The veterinarians examined him, taking X-rays and doing a CT scan.

They found that the joint in his left leg hadn't developed properly, most likely because he didn't have good nutrition after he was taken from his tiger mother. As he continued to eat healthy food at the Safari Park, though, the veterinarians felt that his leg would heal.

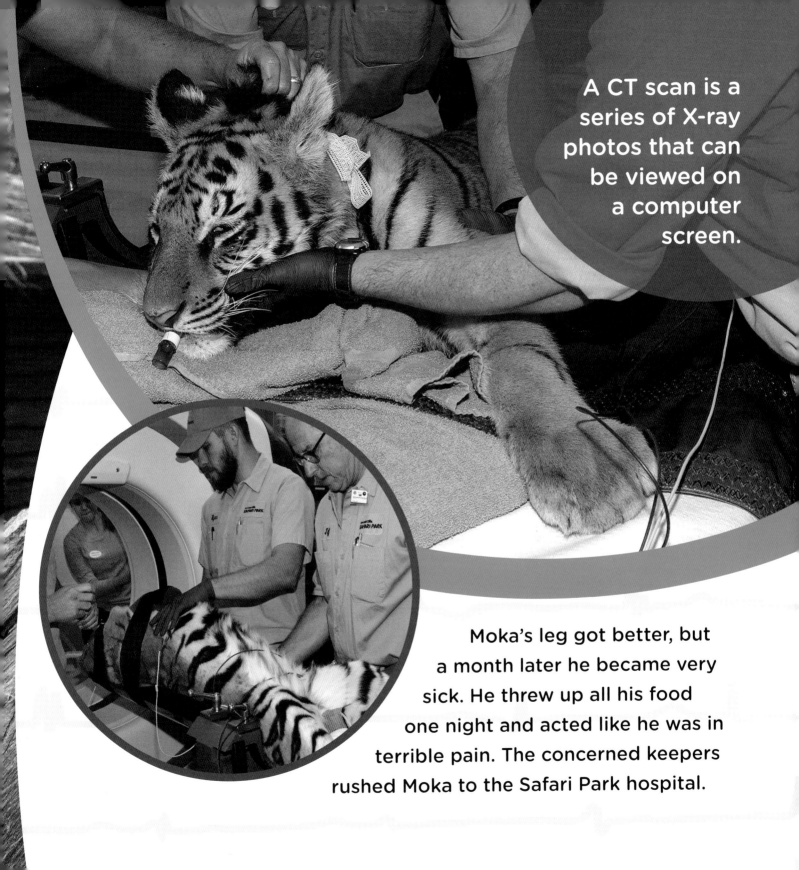

A CT scan is a series of X-ray photos that can be viewed on a computer screen.

Moka's leg got better, but a month later he became very sick. He threw up all his food one night and acted like he was in terrible pain. The concerned keepers rushed Moka to the Safari Park hospital.

Moka had a ball of food in his stomach that he couldn't digest. Using X-rays, the veterinarians saw that his stomach wasn't where it should be. It had moved too close to his lungs through a big hole in his diaphragm. To save his life, veterinarians operated on Moka to remove the food, repair the hole, and move the stomach back to where it belonged.

The veterinarians thought that if Moka hadn't been rescued from the smugglers, he wouldn't have received proper medical care. He most likely would have died at a very young age because of his health issues.

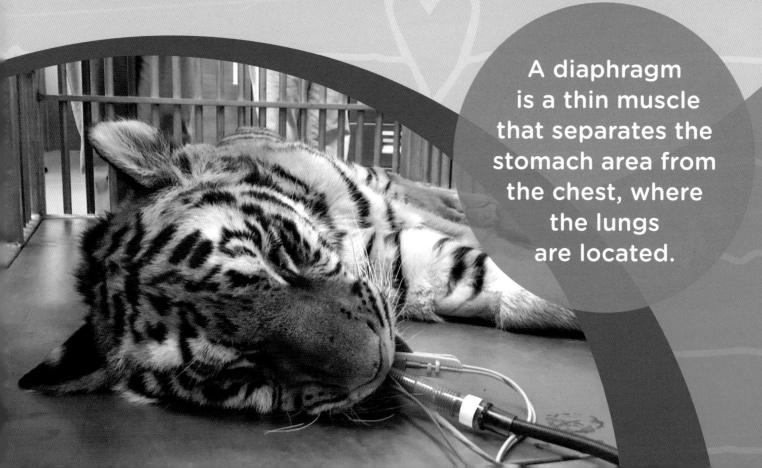

A diaphragm is a thin muscle that separates the stomach area from the chest, where the lungs are located.

Rakan missed Moka very much.

Moka spent a week at the hospital and then recovered for two more weeks in his Tiger Trail bedroom. He and Rakan missed each other very much! When the cubs were finally reunited, they wrestled and played chase, just like they did before Moka got sick.

Growing Up

The cubs grew and matured, acting more and more like adult tigers every day. At nearly a year old, Moka weighed 132 pounds. He was now much bigger than Rakan, who weighed only 117 pounds.

Rakan is a Sumatran tiger—the smallest tiger species. Moka's ancestors are the largest tiger species: Bengal and Amur tigers.

Moka and Rakan were still like brothers as well as best friends. Life was good for them with their comfortable home, healthy food, and keepers who loved them. Plus, their days were spent playing together. They especially liked splashing in their pond, although they continued to tackle and trip each other as they raced through bushes, down hills, and over logs.

The cubs didn't know it, but their lives were about to change forever.

A New Life for Moka and Rakan

On a warm June afternoon, Moka and Rakan played with each other for the last time. When male tigers become adults, they typically don't live together anymore. Because the cubs were nearly grown up, it was time for them to go their separate ways.

The next morning, Moka was moved to a new home— a wildlife sanctuary called Lions Tigers & Bears, where he will live for the rest of his life. Rakan stayed at the Safari Park. Keepers hope that someday, he will become a father to help save his Sumatran tiger species.

Nola

PHOTO BY RYOKO CHONAN

When Moka left, Rakan missed him terribly, although now he is friends with other tigers. At the wildlife sanctuary, Moka met a white tiger named Nola. They won't have cubs together but they are best friends.

Thanks to the many people who rescued Moka from wildlife traffickers and saved his life, Moka is thriving in his new home! Even though Moka and Rakan now live apart, the tiger buddies were there for each other when they needed a friend the most.

Fun Facts about Tigers

Male Amur tigers are the largest big cats in the world. But male African lions are the second largest big cats and weigh more than the other tiger subspecies.

Each tiger has its own unique stripe pattern, much like a human fingerprint.

AMUR

BENGAL

There are six living subspecies of tigers. They live in different habitats: forests, grasslands, and even mangrove swamps.

A tiger's tail is about three feet long and helps it balance when making tight turns.

Tigers are the only cats that are completely striped. Even their skin has stripes!

Tigers are carnivores, which means they only eat meat.

Tigers take down their prey by quietly stalking them until they are close enough to pounce with their sharp claws and large teeth.

Unlike most cats, tigers are excellent swimmers.

INDOCHINESE

SUMATRAN

MALAYAN

SOUTH CHINA

Cubs stay with their mother for about two years until they are ready to hunt on their own.

Tigers are solitary animals. They are only with other tigers during mating or when raising cubs.

Amur tigers can weigh up to 660 pounds.

Where Tigers Live in the World

RUSSIA

MONGOLIA

CHINA

INDIA

SOUTHEAST ASIA

Bay of Bengal

Indian Ocean

MALAYSIA

INDONESIA

Pacific Ocean

**ALL TIGERS ARE ENDANGERED!
THERE ARE FEWER THAN 5,000 LEFT IN THE WILD.**

Threats to Tigers:

Poaching for their fur and body parts

Habitat loss for farming and towns

Deforestation for palm oil plantations in Indonesia and Malaysia

Illegal pet trade

Shortage of prey animals

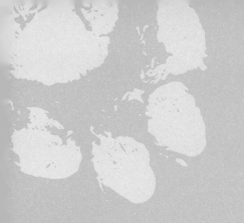

How You Can Help:

To learn how you can be a superhero for tigers
and other wildlife as well as help lead
the fight against extinction, visit:

endextinction.org

and

sandiegozookids.org/save-animals

Learn about Moka and Nola's home at:

lionstigersandbears.org

Learn more about stopping wildlife trafficking at:

wildlifetraffickingalliance.org
fws.gov/international/wildlife-trafficking/

and

traffic.org

Ten Things You and Your Family Can Do to Help Wildlife:

1. Learn about the local wildlife that lives in or near your community.

2. Create your own wildlife habitat by planting native bushes, flowers, and trees in your yard. You can put up a bird feeder, too.

3. Keep your cats indoors so they stay safe and don't hurt local wildlife, such as birds, lizards, and small mammals.

4. Tell your friends and family not to purchase products made from threatened trees and plants, marine organisms, or wild animals when traveling abroad.

5. Put trash that can't be recycled in a garbage can so it doesn't end up harming wildlife or traveling to the ocean.

6. Recycle paper products, glass bottles, cans, and plastic, and say "no" to plastic bottles, straws, lids, and cutlery.

7. Use a reusable water bottle.

8. Take your own reusable bags to the grocery store.

9. Volunteer to be a "citizen scientist" on **wildwatchkenya.org** to help researchers identify wildlife in photos taken on trail cameras (with your parents' permission).

10. Find out more about how climate change is affecting our planet and share this information with the people in your life.